Copyright 2012

Author: Rachel Durchslag & Jackie Payne

Designed by Stacey Gorecki

Editor: Kris McCoy

Printed by CreateSpace

ISBN-13: 978-1468130744

A Girl's Guide To Climbing
Mt. Kilimanjaro

What You Need To Know and Bring
To Have a Wonderful and Comfortable Climb

Table of Contents

About Us

Rachel Durchslag is the Executive Director of the Chicago Alliance Against Sexual Exploitation, a nonprofit dedicated to ending the perpetration of sexual exploitation and harm through prevention, community engagement, legal advocacy, and policy peform. In her spare time, she is a fitness instructor. When not working, Rachel loves finding motorcycle adventures throughout the United States.

Jackie Payne is an advocate for positive change in the areas of fitness and recreation. As a manager, she leads a team of staff for the Chicago Park District on the south side of Chicago and is working to develop programs that help people of all ages bring health and fitness into their lives. She also has been a fitness instructor and personal trainer for the YMCA for the past six years. If she's not working, she is running, teaching Turbo Kick, sleeping, or shopping. Jackie lives in Chicago with her husband, Rafael.

Introduction

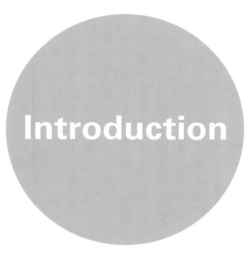

"There were so many great experiences physically, mentally, and spiritually, and there is no doubt that we both gained a tremendous amount from the mountain."

In our own words, here is what brought us to the mountain and, ultimately, to write this guide:

Rachel:

The year 2011 seemed to be a hard one for many people in my life. Whether their challenges (and my own) emerged from work, health issues, friendships, or romances, it seemed that 2011 was a year of personal struggle and self-reflection, as well as self-growth. With an abundance of metaphorical "climbing," 2011 also seemed like the perfect time to climb a literal mountain. Always fascinated with Africa, I decided that I would attempt Mt. Kilimanjaro.

Climbing Kilimanjaro appealed to me for many reasons: it's not a technical climb, it can be done within a week, and you get the amazing experience of truly being on the top of Africa. And then there were the things that I couldn't have anticipated before I went — the opportunity to meet people from around the world, the gift of physical challenges to overcome, and the most amazing night skies I will probably ever see in my lifetime.

My experience was a wonderful one, but there were definitely a few things I would love to have known before I went that would have made the trip that much more enjoyable. That is why Jackie and I decided to create this guide—to ensure that your climb is the best it can be. We hope it is useful as you prepare to summit the fourth-tallest mountain in the world.

Jackie:

Over the last five years, there were many opportunities for Rachel and me to meet (we both attended the same graduate program, had several mutual friends, and worked at the local YMCA), but we really didn't get to know each other until we started training together almost two years ago. Through fitness, Rachel and I developed a friendship. During this time, we were both experiencing transitions in our lives, and the idea of going away to clear our heads was in both of our hearts. Rachel mentioned the idea of climbing Mt. Kilimanjaro one wintery January morning while we were working out, and while I hadn't ever thought of doing it myself, the chance to (1) go to Africa, (2) do something exciting and physically challenging, and (3) experience the metaphorical significance of climbing a mountain made the opportunity hard to refuse.

And it was an amazing trip! There were so many great experiences physically, mentally, and spiritually, and there is no doubt that we both gained a tremendous amount from the mountain. Though we did prepare well for the trip (read books, exercised, got shots, etc.), if asked what I would do differently to make the trip better, I can definitely think of a few suggestions. And it was being unprepared for some of the unpleasant surprises on the mountain that served as the motivation to write this book.

Here are a few things to consider as you plan your trip:

Choosing your travel partner(s):

It is important to think carefully about whom you want next to you on the mountain. You will face physical and emotional challenges that will push you in new and unfamiliar ways, and you will most likely need emotional support at different times during your climb, so make sure you feel quite comfortable with the person you are going with. Also, it is a good idea to go with someone else who is around the same fitness level as you. That way neither of you will feel frustrated having to stop or go more slowly than the other would like.

If you go with a larger group, try to keep the overall group as small as possible as it might be frustrating to have to accommodate different fitness levels in terms of pace, taking breaks, etc. The smaller the group, the easier it is to establish a rhythm during your time on the mountain.

As you and your friend(s) are preparing for your trip, it is a good idea to coordinate your packing. There is no need for multiple people to bring the same first-aid supplies, spices for your food, or air freshener to help with unpleasant toilet outings. The less you bring with you, the less you need to schlep back home. So coordinate packing wisely!

Safety:

When we envisioned our trip to Kilimanjaro, we imagined we would be two of the few people hiking on the mountain. In reality, there were at least two hundred people on the same path we were hiking (the Machame path). Though the amount of people didn't allow for the "isolated in nature" feeling we were hoping for, it did mean that we never felt unsafe as women traveling with a large group of men (our porters and guides). It also meant that there were a ton of people to meet (which we usually did while waiting in line for the bathroom). And though you will not have to fear for your physical safety with others, it is always a good idea to carry your passport and money with you at all times and not leave them unattended at camp.

Transform your climb into a fundraiser:

Though raising money for a charity is probably not your primary motivation to climb Kilimanjaro, since you are going to climb the mountain anyway, you might as well use it as an opportunity to raise funds for something you believe in.

Rachel:

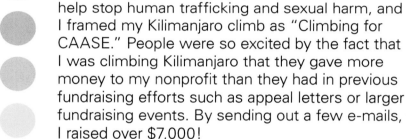 In 2006, I founded a nonprofit called the Chicago Alliance Against Sexual Exploitation (CAASE) to help stop human trafficking and sexual harm, and I framed my Kilimanjaro climb as "Climbing for CAASE." People were so excited by the fact that I was climbing Kilimanjaro that they gave more money to my nonprofit than they had in previous fundraising efforts such as appeal letters or larger fundraising events. By sending out a few e-mails, I raised over $7,000!

Jackie:

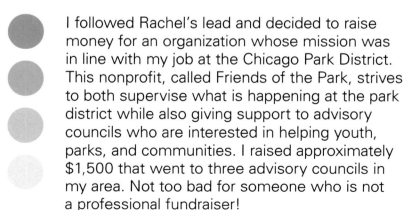 I followed Rachel's lead and decided to raise money for an organization whose mission was in line with my job at the Chicago Park District. This nonprofit, called Friends of the Park, strives to both supervise what is happening at the park district while also giving support to advisory councils who are interested in helping youth, parks, and communities. I raised approximately $1,500 that went to three advisory councils in my area. Not too bad for someone who is not a professional fundraiser!

To facilitate fundraising, we used the website www.razoo.com. Though they take a percentage of the proceeds as a fee for their service, the cost of using the website is on the lower end of what other websites charge.

Additionally, before we left, we held a fundraising event at a local bar that agreed to donate 10 percent of the night's proceeds to the charities we were supporting. It was great to have a night that served as both a fundraiser and a send-off for the climb.

Training

"Though the mountain challenged our physical ability every day, since we had put sufficient time into training, we never felt completely fatigued or overwhelmed."

In the books we read about physically preparing for the climb, it seemed the authors did not properly emphasize the importance of exercise and physical training, concentrating instead on potential altitude-related problems. While the altitude certainly played a role in making our journey challenging, we were extremely grateful that we had put time and energy into getting into the best possible shape before the climb. Though the mountain challenged our physical ability every day, since we had put sufficient time into training, we never felt completely fatigued or overwhelmed.

Here is what we would recommend in terms of training before your climb:

Build muscular strength: Starting 6-8 weeks or more before your trip, work out all major muscle groups (legs, back, chest, biceps, triceps, and abdominals) at least two times a week for 30-45 minutes.

Jackie:

- Don't worry about being fancy with your exercises; sticking to the basics will get you where you need to be for climbing Mt. Kilimanjaro.

For legs: Place particular emphasis on leg exercises that target the gluteals, hamstrings, and quadriceps. Do 12-15 repetitions of leg exercises three times for one full set.

While squats, wall sits, hamstring curls, and dead lifts will help with most of the hiking up the mountain, with both of us being under 5'5", there were definitely times when we needed to use our hands and upper body to lift ourselves up to reach the next part of a trail or to get secure footing (or to complete less glamorous tasks like stuffing sleeping bags into very tight packs). Therefore, work on your upper body as well.

For the upper body (chest, back, and arms): We recommend push-ups (30-40 repetitions), which target your chest, and triceps and pull-ups (3 sets of 6 full pull-ups or 3 sets of 15-25 assisted pull-ups), which are great for biceps and back. Again, you can't beat the basics!

Rachel:

I worked out for several months with a personal trainer before the climb. Though it is definitely not necessary to work with a trainer, mine helped me focus on exercises to strengthen the muscles I would use most frequently on the mountain. He also made me face my fear of the Stair Master.

I hated the Stair Master. I would complain about having to do even a couple of minutes on the dreaded machine. But my trainer made it very clear that the more time I spent on the Stair Master, the greater the likelihood that I would succeed with my climb. When I started my training, I could last four minutes on the climber. By the time I left for Kilimanjaro, I could do an hour without holding onto the handrails. If you can get to the point where you can do a similar workout, you will be prepared for your climb. I also recommend walking at the highest incline on the treadmill for an hour. You can switch off between the two machines, striving for a total of four hours of cardio a week.

Jackie:

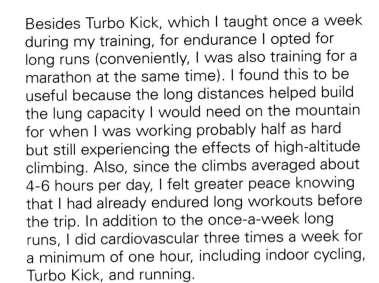

Besides Turbo Kick, which I taught once a week during my training, for endurance I opted for long runs (conveniently, I was also training for a marathon at the same time). I found this to be useful because the long distances helped build the lung capacity I would need on the mountain for when I was working probably half as hard but still experiencing the effects of high-altitude climbing. Also, since the climbs averaged about 4-6 hours per day, I felt greater peace knowing that I had already endured long workouts before the trip. In addition to the once-a-week long runs, I did cardiovascular three times a week for a minimum of one hour, including indoor cycling, Turbo Kick, and running.

Another helpful way to physically prepare for the climb is to learn to rock climb or even simply train on a rock-climbing wall. While you won't be doing any belaying/serious rock climbing on Kilimanjaro, our minimal previous experience with rock climbing (knowing to push with the legs rather than pull with the hands) proved useful on the mountain.

Lastly, do not forget about your abs! We cannot stress enough the importance of building a strong core. It is the basis for all movement in the body.

Jackie:

I would also recommend wall sits, which will greatly help the unpleasant experience of squatting in the drop toilets. Wall sits are done by squatting with your back against a wall with your legs bent at a 90-degree angle, keeping your knees above your ankles and pressing your back to the wall. Hold this position for 30, 60, or 90 seconds. Practicing wall sits would have helped my legs and my anxiety and possibly lessened the time I spent in the drop toilet!

Packing for the Climb

"For both of us, even more stressful than physically training for the hike was figuring out what to pack."

For both of us, even more stressful than physically training for the hike was figuring out what to pack. There are many websites and books that can help you with your packing list (we recommend Climbing Mount Kilimanjaro by Stephen Carmichael, Susan Stoddard, Rick Ridgeway, and Neville Shulman) and most guide companies will have packing recommendations on their websites. Since these resources already provide basic packing recommendations, we won't repeat that information here. However, there are certain things we are definitely glad we had or wished we had more of that were not covered on most of these lists. Below are a few things you might not think about bringing, but you will be very glad to have with you on the mountain.

Clothes

One thing to note is that temperatures on the mountain can fluctuate. During the day, the mountain can be quite warm, with temperatures dropping significantly after the sun has set. The weather also gets colder the higher you are on the mountain, so make sure you plan to wear many layers every day.

- *Comfortable sleeping socks:* We both brought socks infused with aloe vera. Our feet were quite grateful for this treat at the end of the day.

- *PJs:* Make sure to bring one to two items to sleep in every night. The last thing you'll want is to sleep in your dirty and dusty hiking clothes.

- *Underwear:* There are a couple of underwear options for the mountain—one is quite environmentally friendly and the other is much more convenient. The environmentally friendly option is to purchase a few pairs of ExOfficio underwear, which are made of mostly nylon and are great for absorbing sweat and potentially unpleasant odors. The other option is not so environmentally friendly—buy seven pairs of cheap cotton underwear and throw a pair away each day. Though we went the environmentally friendly route, in all honesty, we wished we had opted for other.

- *An extra pair of shoes:* When you are done hiking for the day, the last thing you will want is to wear your hiking boots around camp. Plan to bring a pair of gym shoes or Tevas (which you can wear with socks) for your time in camp.

- *Tank tops and t-shirts:* Though it is important to have proper hiking gear during the day, at camp you will want to have a few cotton shirts that you can change into.

- *Fleece jacket:* BRING ONE! You will use it constantly.

- *Clothes with pockets:* More pockets means more ways to organize all the things you will carry during the day.

- *Winter coat:* You will need a really heavy coat for the summit. Purchase something that one would wear to ski. Try to bring a coat with big pockets INSIDE. During the summit, you will want to keep your water bottle inside of your coat to prevent the water from freezing.

- *Winter hat:* Made of wool or fleece for nighttime wear.

Rachel:

> I brought only a balaclava and wished I had a smaller winter hat to wear around camp.

- *Glove liners and warm gloves:* You will use both.

- *Sunglasses:* The sun is strong on the mountain; you'll be happy you brought these.

- *Wool socks and liners:* Bring at least three pairs. We loved Smartwool.

- *Baseball cap*: In addition to keeping your hair out of the way, the baseball cap can be a great sun deflector and keep you from getting headaches due to squinting or too much heat exposure.

Jackie:

> I also used a couple of bandanas to tie around my neck. Not only did I get to pretend to be a cowgirl, they were also great for wiping my nose or as a mask when using the bathroom.

Gear

- *A duffle for your clothes:* Whatever bag you choose for your personal items on the mountain will be what you will physically have next to you in your tent. To maximize tent space, try to bring the smallest bag possible that will fit all of your items. If you want easy access to your things, we would recommend bringing a small duffle instead of a backpack since a duffle makes accessing clothes and gear easier than rummaging through a vertical backpack. Since the porter will carry your bag inside a tarp bag, it does not necessarily help him or her to carry your things if you bring a backpack, and the backpack will only make it harder for you to organize and access your things.

- *Camelback and water bottle:* Camelbacks make hiking much easier since you do not have to stop constantly to drink water. They are especially nice on the summit since they fit easily within your jacket. In addition to a camelback, bring a sturdy water bottle that you are not attached to since the plastic will most likely become discolored due to iodine.

- *Swiss Army knife:* These are great for opening snack packs, cutting mole skin, slicing pills in half, and dealing with other unexpected challenges that may arise.

- *Water bottle insulator:* This will help prevent your water from freezing on the summit.

- *Pillow:* Many camping stores and websites sell travel pillows that can be blown up and then deflated for easy packing. Having a pillow to rest your head on makes sleeping a lot easier.

- *Headlamp:* You will look silly but will be happy to have this for reading at night, navigating outings to the bathroom in the dark, and for the summit night.

- *Gaiters* (protection that loops over your boot and protects the bottom of your pants): WEAR GAITORS! They keep dust and stones out of your shoes and will help keep you slightly less dirty. If you do not want to purchase them, see if you can rent them from your tour company. Or, if you do purchase them and know that you will not use them again, donate them to a porter.

- *Walking sticks:* We did not use these for the majority of the trip, but they were good on steep declines. If you are not sure if you are going to like walking with the sticks, it might be a good idea to rent them instead of spending a lot of money purchasing a new pair. You can usually rent them from your chosen outfitter.

Jackie:

> I used walking sticks going downhill because my knees were sore. Luckily, I had a friend who loaned me her sticks. In my opinion, although they helped my descent after reaching the summit, I would have been fine without them. After a few hours, they became more of a nuisance.

Extras

- *Ziplock bags:* Tons of them! You will be amazed at all the uses you will find for these. While we recommend bringing a variety of sizes, we used the one-gallon bags most frequently.

- *Garbage bags:* Definitely bring a few full-sized garbage bags on your trip. They help keep clothes dry, are great dirty-laundry bags, and can be used to collect garbage while on the mountain.

- *Great book(s):* You will have a lot of down time while on the mountain. It was rare that we arrived at camp any later than 3:00 p.m., and we were then left with the entire day with nothing to do. A great book helped pass the time.

Rachel:

> I actually brought my Kindle and charged it with a solar charger I kept on the outside of my pack. I went for the cheapest charger, which was evident in its unreliability. I would recommend purchasing a solar charger to charge your phone and camera, but I would also recommend spending the money to purchase one of better quality.

- *Journal:* Your experience climbing the mountain is something that you will probably want to capture in a journal. Every day will be completely different not only in terms of environment but in the lessons the mountain teaches. Journaling will help you hold on to what you experience and the ways you will grow.

- *Inspirational quotes/passages from friends:* We had no doubt that climbing Kilimanjaro would be one of the most challenging things we had ever done, both physically and emotionally. And we knew there would be moments on the mountain when we would be grateful for some words of inspiration.

Rachel:

Before the trip, I reached out to my close friends and asked them to e-mail me a quote, poem, or passage that helped them get through challenges in their lives. The response was overwhelming. I ended up bringing thirty pages of inspirational text from my friends; I read every word and took much comfort in what my friends shared. On the summit, I even hiked with the printouts in my backpack as an additional source of inspiration.

- *Sudoku/puzzles/crosswords:* These are good for downtime at camp.

- *Ear plugs:* Camp is noisy! There were about two hundred people at each of our campsites, and many stayed up much later than we did. Ear plugs didn't ensure total silence, but they significantly helped mute the noise at night.

- *Alarm:* You will need to get yourself up in the morning, so an alarm is quite useful. Many digital watches have an alarm function which is sufficient.

- *Phone:* There are places on the mountain where you will get some reception. Though we were excited to be "unplugged" during our trip, it was really nice to get to text friends and family to let them know that we made it to the summit.

Jackie:

> Before your trip, make sure to update your phone plan a couple weeks before you leave (so if your phone company needs to send you an international phone, you will get it). Also update your e-mail and text plan to include international options and avoid huge additional; charges.

- *iPod:* It is nice to have music on the mountain to listen to either when hiking or when trying to fall asleep at night.

- *Business cards:* On the mountain, you will meet people from all over the world. Bring business cards so you can easily exchange information. If you do not have a card, you can always make a free one at www.VistaPrint.com.

- *Disposable camera:* Bring this for the summit in case your camera battery runs out of juice! It's also a good idea to bring an extra camera battery.

Medicine
- *Advil:* This helps with muscle soreness and headaches from altitude.

Jackie:

> I took two Advil every morning to help prevent muscle pain. Surprisingly, I rarely got sick or headaches!

- *Pepto-Bismol:* Your stomach might do some funky things on the mountain. It's good to be prepared.

- *NO SLEEPING PILLS:* Even if sleeping is a challenge (and it most likely will be), DO NOT take a sleeping pill. It will make you more vulnerable to altitude sickness.

- *Cough drops:* These are like little pieces of heaven on the mountain. They are especially lovely on the summit. Also, bring enough for your guides. They will be grateful.

- *High-level sunblock for your face and body:* The sun will be much stronger than it feels. We used 90 SPF and still got sun.

Rachel:

> I forgot to put sunscreen on my lips, and my bottom lip got horribly burnt. In addition to sunscreen, I wish I had brought lip balm with SPF protection.

- *Pills for altitude sickness:* Ask your doctor for more information. These helped us a lot.

- *Bug spray with 100 percent DEET:* Luckily we did not have to use our bug spray much on the mountain since it was the dry season. After the first day, there are barely any live things (bugs or animals) on Kilimanjaro, and we were able to put the bug spray away until the last day of the climb. Still, we were happy to have that level of protection just in case.

Jackie:

The travel clinic where I got my shots recommended a bug spray with a minimum of 25 percent DEET. I bought a bug spray with 34 percent DEET and used it one summer night in Chicago and was still eaten alive! So, I went back to the store and bought the 100 percent DEET spray. Because we encountered so few bugs due to the dry season, I probably would have been fine with the 34 percent DEET. However, for peace of mind, get the 100 percent.

- *Aloe lotion:* This feels wonderful on burnt skin.

Jackie:

The aloe lotion was great when my nose and upper lip became dry and irritated from all the nose blowing.

Hygiene

"Though we found extensive lists of things to bring for the trip, we quickly realized that many of these packing lists did not take into consideration certain items that women might want."

Maintaining a sense of cleanliness while on the mountain is definitely a challenge. Though we found extensive lists of things to bring for the trip, we quickly realized that many of these packing lists did not take into consideration certain items that women might want. Here are a few things you can bring to help you feel as clean as possible:

- *Body wipes:* These are much larger than baby wipes and are the closest thing you will have to a shower on the mountain. We used Fresh Body + Bath (available on Amazon) and loved them. We used 1-2 a day and that was exactly what we needed.

- *Light body mist:* This versatile product can do many things, from helping with the odor in the bathroom (see future chapter) to just giving yourself a fresher smell each day.

- *Nail brush/clippers:* Clippers are great for keeping your nails short, but more importantly, clippers that have the dirt scraper will be essential for getting dirt out from under your nails (which was a surprising challenge). A nail brush will also help your hands feel clean, making such things as eating, putting in or taking out contacts, taking pills, or filling your water bottle more sanitary.

- *Comb/brush:* To help remove some of the dust and dirt and to remove the potential for unwanted tangles and dreadlocks.

Jackie:

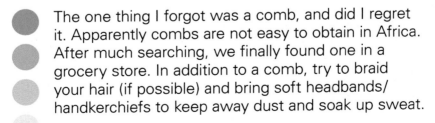 The one thing I forgot was a comb, and did I regret it. Apparently combs are not easy to obtain in Africa. After much searching, we finally found one in a grocery store. In addition to a comb, try to braid your hair (if possible) and bring soft headbands/handkerchiefs to keep away dust and soak up sweat.

- *Anti-bacterial wipes:* These were great to use before every meal and after the bathroom. Bring a ton! We went through at least seventy wipes on the mountain.

- *Hand sanitizer:* You will use this all the time. It really helps you feel better about touching food during meals and/or eating a snack from your backpack.

- *Liquid soap:* The soap our porters gave us for hand washing never seemed to leave us feeling clean. We would advise bringing a little of your own environmentally friendly liquid soap, especially if you are putting in or taking out contacts.

- *Face astringent with cotton balls:* A wonderful pleasure to really get into the deep pores of your skin at the end of the day. It will be an amazing (and slightly frightening) experience to see the amount of dirt that collects on your skin.

- *Q-Tips:* Bring them to clean your ears and nose, the latter of which can get really dry and uncomfortable.

Rachel:

> Your nose may get dry, crusty, and even slightly painful, and it helps to put a little Neosporin on a Q-Tip and clean the inside of your nostrils. It worked wonders for us.

- *Small compact mirror:* You don't really need anything larger (and might not want anything larger because it will show you how truly dirty you are!), but a small compact mirror was great for putting in contacts and to check out the occasional painful or dry area.

- *Items for handling contacts:* Make sure to bring a contact case, solution, and a back-up pair of contacts.

Jackie:

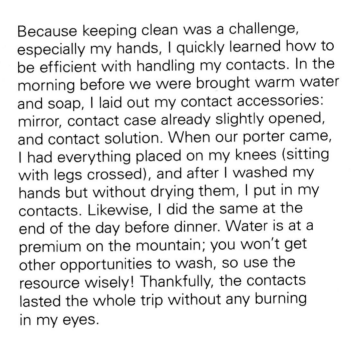

Because keeping clean was a challenge, especially my hands, I quickly learned how to be efficient with handling my contacts. In the morning before we were brought warm water and soap, I laid out my contact accessories: mirror, contact case already slightly opened, and contact solution. When our porter came, I had everything placed on my knees (sitting with legs crossed), and after I washed my hands but without drying them, I put in my contacts. Likewise, I did the same at the end of the day before dinner. Water is at a premium on the mountain; you won't get other opportunities to wash, so use the resource wisely! Thankfully, the contacts lasted the whole trip without any burning in my eyes.

Food

"My snack bag consisted of a Luna Bar, lollipop, Pop Tart (which kind of crumbled but was delicious nonetheless), throat lozenges, and some water flavor packets such as Gatorade and Crystal Lite."

We are the type of people who always travel with snacks both to make sure we have things that will give us energy throughout the day and so that we are not anxiously waiting for the next meal to arrive.

Rachel:

Carrying snacks is especially important for me since, as a vegan, I am frequently in situations where there is nothing I can eat. Though I called the tour company multiple times before I left to make sure that my dietary restrictions could be accommodated (and was told repeatedly that they could), when I got to Kilimanjaro, they had barely prepared vegetarian options, let alone vegan ones. Fortunately, after the first day the cook understood what I could and could not eat and was very accommodating. Unfortunately, protein was almost nonexistent for me outside of peanut butter (I ate more PB&Js on Kilimanjaro than I probably have total in the last ten years). So, bringing extra food really helped. If you are meat eater, there will be plenty of protein for you at every meal.

Dietary restrictions aside, your cook will make more food than you will possibly be able to eat. So know that you will absolutely eat well and never be hungry after a meal. But during the day, outside of lunch, the only food you will have access to is the food you bring, which is why snacks are so important.

Jackie:

I organized my food by pre-packing snack bags for each day on the mountain. My snack bag consisted of a Luna Bar, lollipop, Pop Tart (which kind of crumbled but were delicious nonetheless), throat lozenges, and some water flavor packets such as Gatorade and Crystal Lite.

We would recommend bringing some of the following:

- *Energy bars:* Of all snack options, these are the most important to bring. Clif Bars, Luna Bars, and PowerBars are all great midday snacks to give you energy and help you keep going.

Rachel:

I officially fell in love with GU, made by Clif Bar, on the mountain. On the days when I was struggling with altitude sickness, I could always get down a packet. And they are great for energy.

- *Warm drinks:* You will be offered tea, coffee, and most likely hot chocolate every morning and evening. However, if you have a favorite type of tea or instant coffee, it's a good idea to bring it with you. Also, remember to bring any type of sweetener you may want to use for your hot beverages.

Rachel:

I chose to bring Mate de Coca tea (available on Amazon) since it is known to help with altitude sickness.

Jackie:

> Starbucks instant coffee, powdered vanilla creamer, and Truvia were my staples. As a daily coffee drinker, I felt my coffee needs were satisfied.

- *Iodine:* Even though the cook will boil your water, you can never be too careful with guarding against getting sick. We used iodine in all of our water.

- *Gatorade/Propel/NUUN/anything with electrolytes:* It's good to have some type of supplement to add to your water (both for energy and to hide the taste of the iodine).

- *Small packs of peanut butter:* These are fantastic! You can get them at grocery stores, and they are not much bigger than disposable packs of ketchup/mustard. A good brand is Justin's.

- *Tofu:* There is a brand of tofu (Mori-Nu) that does not need to be refrigerated. The drawback with bringing this product is that the tofu takes up a lot of space. However, if you are vegetarian, it is nice to have a good protein source on the mountain.

- *Oatmeal:* Every morning, our cook made porridge with sugar and vinegar, something we couldn't quite get used to. This is why we were glad that we brought small packets of instant oatmeal to have in the morning.

- *Hummus packs:* We didn't bring these but wish we had; they would have been great as an extra protein source. You can find Wild Garden Hummus Dip packs on Amazon.

- *Small salt/pepper packets:* Though most of the food was delicious, some of it benefited from a bit of seasoning.

Jackie:

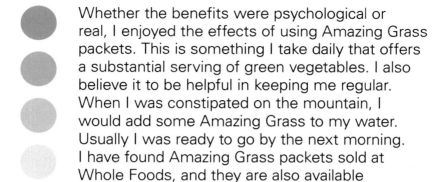

Whether the benefits were psychological or real, I enjoyed the effects of using Amazing Grass packets. This is something I take daily that offers a substantial serving of green vegetables. I also believe it to be helpful in keeping me regular. When I was constipated on the mountain, I would add some Amazing Grass to my water. Usually I was ready to go by the next morning. I have found Amazing Grass packets sold at Whole Foods, and they are also available on Amazon.

Remember to eat a lot on the mountain! Your body will desperately need the energy to get you to the top. Though you will most likely lose your appetite due to altitude, you still need to force yourself to consume calories. And since your body will burn far more calories than usual, you can eat a ton and still find your clothes fitting more loosely after the trip.

Bathroom

"The entire bathroom experience on the mountain took us a bit by surprise..."

The entire bathroom experience on the mountain took us a bit by surprise. We both have done Outward Bound trips and were prepared to squat behind a tree and dig holes to preserve the area. Being in nature, we assumed nature would be where we took care of our elimination needs. Unfortunately, we were not so lucky. Instead of nature, we had to use drop toilets. While you would think it would be a luxury to have toilets on the mountain, we would have preferred the alternative.

Using drop toilets is required on Kilimanjaro, and we wished we had known this beforehand so that we could have taken precautions to make the situation more bearable. Indeed, it was our reflections on the bathroom experience that motivated us to write this book.

Drop toilets are basically holes in the ground of varying depths that collect waste. The long drop toilets are the more tolerable and the short drop toilets are to be avoided as much as possible since the shorter length of the hole adds to the unpleasantness of the experience.

The problems with the drop toilets are the cleanliness and smell. Regardless of size, shape, condition, and newness, every bathroom was unpleasant. Still, there were a few things we did—or wished we had done—to improve the experience.

- *Don't forget toilet paper!* You will need at least 1-2 rolls (and they can double as tissues since your nose will frequently run due to the altitude).

- *BRING AIR FRESHENER!* Any type of air freshener will aid in cutting a bit of the smell and give you at least a slight sense of creating a sanitary space.

- Ask your guides where the best toilets are.

- *Baby wipes:* These were excellent for bathroom time to keep the private areas clean.

- When you encounter a particularly unpleasant bathroom, you can always put scented oil under your nostrils. We tried to do this with scented lotion, but the scent of the lotion wasn't strong enough.

- Get creative in finding places to pee. For example, at one of the campsites, we just couldn't force ourselves to use the toilet and instead hid behind a rain poncho while peeing in daylight.

- Lastly, DO NOT LOOK DOWN AT THE DROP TOILETS!

If you are not used to squatting for long periods of time (as most of us are not), it might be helpful to do some exercises to physically prepare for the toilets. As previously mentioned, we would recommend wall sits. In addition to wall sits, try practicing going to the bathroom without sitting all the way down on your toilet. This should help lessen the anxiety when using the drop toilets and will help your body adjust to engaging your quadriceps and hamstring muscles during bathroom time.

If you are faint of heart and reading this is a deal breaker in your decision to climb, please note that there were some outfitters on the mountain that provided personal bathrooms for their groups. It will cost additional money, but don't let the bathroom experience scare you out of going on the trip. It was probably the most unpleasant part of our climbing experience but also provided a lot of good fun and laughter, and it was during our time queuing for the bathroom that we met many wonderful people from other groups.

Summit

"I kept telling myself that every step was a step closer to not only getting to the top but being able to get back to our camp and sleep. This helped!"

The summit is hard. It doesn't matter how fit you are—if you are not used to expending energy at altitude, you are more than likely going to struggle. Not only will you possibly feel the effects of the altitude, which can manifest as nausea and a headache, but it might be physically challenging to breathe as well. Additionally, since your muscles will not be getting proper oxygen, the physical exertion will feel that much more intense.

Just know that experiencing these symptoms is normal! But definitely read up on altitude sickness before you go so that you will be able to assess if what you are experiencing is serious enough that you should descend immediately.

Though there is little you can do to physically prepare for the altitude on the summit, there are things you can do to help with the overall experience of the ascent:

- *Do what you can to acclimatize:* We opted to spend an extra day on the mountain, which helped us handle the altitude on the summit. We also hiked higher than we camped every day. Though usually the last thing you want to do once you get to camp is to put your boots back on to hike more, trust your guides that this will really help you make it to the summit.

- *Bring snacks that are easy to digest:* Since you will most likely feel nauseated and have trouble eating.

Rachel:

Because of the altitude my stomach didn't want to tolerate solid food. That is why here again I recommend my Kilimanjaro love, GU.

- *Bring a thermos:* We saw other groups drinking hot beverages on the summit, which seemed quite lovely to us. Check with your guides if this is a possibility.

- *Concentrate on just taking one step at a time:* You will summit incredibly slowly. At first we became quite overwhelmed knowing that it would take us 6-8 hours to reach the top. Then we decided to really concentrate on simply putting one foot in front of the other. Concentrating on small successes helped us push through.

Rachel:

> I kept telling myself that every step was a step closer to not only getting to the top but being able to get back to our camp and sleep. This helped!

- *Bring Hot Hands and Hot Toes packs:* These warming packets help lessen the impact of the cold and provide an additional heat source for several hours

- *Keep your water bottles inside your jacket:* Try to keep your water close to your natural body heat when possible.

Jackie:

> I didn't have good pockets on the inside of my coat, and my water froze on the summit climb. As if the summit climb wasn't challenging enough, imagine how hard it was without water.

- *Taking breaks:* Due to the extreme cold, you will not be able to take long breaks on the summit. Be prepared for this, and to help not get too exhausted, concentrate on going slowly.

- *Bring a menstrual pad:* Some women have reported getting their period due to the altitude on the summit. Though this did not happen to us, it might be beneficial to be prepared just in case.

Also, know that at one point it is going to get ridiculously steep on your summit ascent—this means you are almost there!!

Jackie:

As Rachel mentioned before, we climbed the mountain with two hundred other folks on the Machame route. However, that number did not include the few hundred other hikers who were on other routes and summiting at the same time we were. I brought five different signs to take photos with, but there was only one "Congratulations You Are At The Top of Kilimanjaro" sign for the few hundred people summitting. This meant that only one summit photo/group could be taken at a time. Needless to say, I didn't have very much alone time to take photos with my signs, and folks waiting in line were a little restless. In retrospect, I would have opted to take just a couple signs for my photos so as not to monopolize the one summit sign.

Rituals on the Mountain

"We created daily rituals that greatly enriched
our experience and helped us stay in a place
of gratitude and awe."

Throughout the entirety of our trip, we repeatedly expressed our appreciation for being able to travel to Africa—to see the amazing cultures and experience such great adventures. We both kept journals to the capture what we experienced and learned each day. In addition to journaling, we also created daily rituals that greatly enriched our experience and helped us stay in a place of gratitude and awe.

- *Five miracles:* Before dinner each night, we committed to share five miracles that we witnessed or experienced that day. Examples included beautiful sites we saw, moments when we felt proud of what we had accomplished physically, and amazing people that we met. The only rule we made was that we couldn't repeat a miracle day to day, which made us be open to seeing miracles in places we would not normally look.

- *Daily lesson:* In addition to our five miracles, we would share a daily lesson. These lessons were usually personal discoveries about ourselves or insights into life challenges we left in Chicago.

- *Intentions:* Each day on the mountain, as we began our climb, we would put forth an intention about how we wanted the day to go, what we wanted to focus on, and/or what we wanted to put out into the universe. We came to the mountain facing many challenges both personally and professionally, and setting a daily intention helped us transform the climb into both a learning opportunity and a meditation for what we were experiencing.

- *Quotes:* We found certain quotes to be inspirational during our journey.

Rachel:

Of all the wonderful thoughts and poems my friends shared with me, two truly stood out and helped me reach the summit. The first was actually a quote from the Harry Potter series when Dumbledore is speaking to Harry and says, "It is **our choices...**that show what we truly are, far more than **our abilities....**"

This quote resonated with me because it reminded me that it was my choice to actually climb the mountain, not whether or not I made it to the summit, that was of most importance.

The second was the following quote from Jeanette Winterson: "Whatever it is that pulls the pin, that pushes you past the boundaries of your own life into brief and total beauty, even for a moment, it is enough."

Leaving It Behind

"Leaving extra clothes and supplies behind also helped make room for the gifts and souvenirs I brought back to the United States."

Jackie:

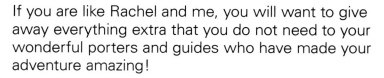

If you are like Rachel and me, you will want to give away everything extra that you do not need to your wonderful porters and guides who have made your adventure amazing!

Purchasing the proper equipment for our mountain climb felt both daunting and expensive. After my first trip to REI where I spent over $400, I knew I was going to have to get creative and resourceful with the rest of my equipment needs as I had a tight budget. So I went to my local thrift store and found several ski jackets that were perfect for the climb and summit day—they were all under twenty bucks! I also found fleece pants and rain gear there. I then had the clothes dry-cleaned, and was good to go.

Not only did shopping at the thrift store help curb some of my costs, it made it easy to give much of my gear away to our porters (many of whom were without proper clothes and supplies such as coats, shirts, hiking boots, etc.). Leaving extra clothes and supplies behind also helped make room for the gifts and souvenirs I brought back to the United States.

Things to note about leaving items behind:

Color/gender: Our porters did not seem to care about the color or intended gender of our items. Many people are in such need of clothes that anything you can share will be used.

Distribution guidance: We looked to our lead guide to help us distribute the clothes we wanted to donate. He was able to tell us which porters needed items the most and also helped us to reward those porters that did exceptional work with these additional gifts.

Some other items to give away:

- *Shirts from your hometown:* It was a great reflection of our city pride to give our guides t-shirts bearing the name "Chicago."

- *Socks and warm clothes:* These are always needed by porters and guides.

- *Extra food:* We used our extra snacks to make goodie bags for the porters at the end of the trip.

Lastly, at the gate you will encounter some local children from the community asking for gifts, food, etc. If you can, have candy, pencils, markers, crayons, pens, or other lightweight items to distribute.

Porters & Tipping

"*Many porters are not able to afford the proper gear to keep themselves warm and safe on Kilimanjaro. Your tips can help them make purchases that, in extreme conditions, might be lifesaving.*"

We were a bit taken aback during our orientation when we learned how much we were expected to tip the porters, cook, and guides. We definitely did not bring an extra $300 each to cover the cost! Had we done better research (i.e., read the tour company's website) before we left, we would have been much more prepared.

Tipping well is really important since your porters and guides are the main reason you are able to climb the mountain. And as you will see, many porters are not able to afford the proper gear to keep themselves warm and safe on Kilimanjaro. Your tips can help them make purchases that, in extreme conditions, might be lifesaving.

Know, however, that you do not have to tip all the porters the same amount. Ask your guides which porters did an especially good job and compensate them accordingly. When we gave our porters their tips, we put the money into small goodie bags in which we also placed our unused snacks, hand warmers, and candies. It was nice to be able to give a bag to each (another good use for Ziplock bags!) rather than simply handing over cash.

Speaking of porters, really take the opportunity to get to know those in your group. We attempted to learn as much Swahili as possible while climbing so that we could at least say "thank you," "good morning," and "hello" in their language.

Here are some words that we learned that helped us communicate:

Hello: Jambo
Thank you: Asante
Slowly: Pole pole
How's it going?: Habari
It's going well: Nzuri
Friend: Rafiki
Goodbye: Kwaheri
Yes: Ndio
No: Hapana
Welcome: Karibu
Good morning : Habari ya asubuhi
Good afternoon: Habari ya mchana
Good evening: Habari ya jioni
Sorry: Samahani
Please: Tafadhali

Many tour companies support the Porters Association, an organization that helps ensure better working conditions for the porters on the mountain. Try to pick a tour company that supports this group.

And finally, if you have the time, treat your porters and guides to a beer at the end of the climb when you are in town. It is a great way to say thank you and to celebrate all that they have helped you accomplish.

After the Climb

"The challenge is holding on to how you grew physically, emotionally, and spiritually once you are back in the hustle of everyday life."

Climbing Kilimanjaro is transformative, and you will be forever changed by what you experience on the mountain. The challenge, of course, is holding on to how you grew physically, emotionally, and spiritually once you are back in the hustle of everyday life. To help you incorporate what you learn on the mountain into life after the climb, we have a few suggestions.

Rachel:

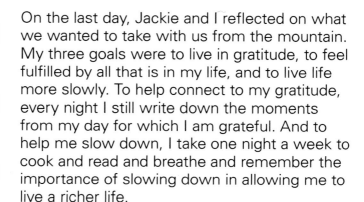

On the last day, Jackie and I reflected on what we wanted to take with us from the mountain. My three goals were to live in gratitude, to feel fulfilled by all that is in my life, and to live life more slowly. To help connect to my gratitude, every night I still write down the moments from my day for which I am grateful. And to help me slow down, I take one night a week to cook and read and breathe and remember the importance of slowing down in allowing me to live a richer life.

Jackie and I also have become accountability partners for each other. We still ask each other what our intentions are for a particular day or week, and we help remind each other of all that we gained from what we accomplished.

Jackie:

I have continued the five-miracles-a-day practice and do not allow myself to repeat any miracles from day to day. This has taught me to include miracles that aren't what I would normally label "pleasant" but nonetheless remind me to be present (like someone honking at me, gaffing at an important meeting, etc.) Instead of judging the act, I list it as a miracle if it keeps me in the present moment and helps me challenge myself to see what significance or lesson I can take from the experience.

We hope this guide will help you feel more prepared and secure on the mountain. You are about to have a truly amazing adventure, and the more comfortable you can be, the more you will enjoy the magic of Kilimanjaro. Have fun, laugh frequently, push yourself, and celebrate your bravery for choosing to climb the tallest mountain in Africa.

Things to Pack

○ _____

○ _____

○ _____

○ _____

○ _____

○ _____

○ _____

○ _____

○ _____

○ _____

○ _____

○ _____

○ _____

○ _____

○ _____

○ _____

○ _____

○ _____

○ _____

Things to Pack

○ _____
○ _____
○ _____
○ _____
○ _____
○ _____
○ _____
○ _____
○ _____
○ _____
○ _____
○ _____
○ _____
○ _____
○ _____
○ _____
○ _____
○ _____
○ _____
○ _____

Things to Pack

○ _____
○ _____
○ _____
○ _____
○ _____
○ _____
○ _____
○ _____
○ _____
○ _____
○ _____
○ _____
○ _____
○ _____
○ _____
○ _____
○ _____
○ _____
○ _____

Things to Pack

○ _____
○ _____
○ _____
○ _____
○ _____
○ _____
○ _____
○ _____
○ _____
○ _____
○ _____
○ _____
○ _____
○ _____
○ _____
○ _____
○ _____
○ _____
○ _____

Notes

Notes

Notes

Notes

Made in the USA
Monee, IL
07 July 2021

73089697R10040